by
Margaret Islander

©1991
Islander Sewing Systems™
Highland, Michigan

Revised Edition

Acknowledgement is due "Patternmaking for Fashion Design" by Helen Joseph Armstrong (Harper & Row) for fresh insight in refining dart calculation. I highly recommend this book to anyone interested in pursuing pattern drafting in its totality.

Published by
Janet & Company, Inc
Highland, Michigan

ISBN 0-9629081-1-8
Revised 1991
Reprinted 2005, 2007 & 2009

Printed in China

Dedication...

To my close friend and staunch supporter, Ingrid Wikstrom, to Kay Marie Kreitman for her expertise in technical aspects, to Marisa Robles, my original pattern drafting instructor, from whose instructions this system has evolved over the years, and to the hundreds of wonderful students who have successfully used these methods and urged me to publish them, my love and sincerest gratitude.

Dear Friends,

As I welcome you to this wonderful realm of pattern drafting, my thoughts quite naturally go back to the time I was first introduced to it myself. Having pursued almost every avenue of home and couture sewing I decided next to look into the designer courses taught for the clothing industry. I began with Pattern Drafting. The first evening in that class is still crystal clear in my memory. A whole new world had opened up. Not since childhood had I felt such excitement and anticipation! Watching a plain sheet of paper evolve into an actual pattern in my own hands was sheer magic! Many years have passed since then. My thirst for knowledge in this field is and always has been insatiable. Yet, even now, the sense of creativity, power and wonder I found in Pattern Drafting stands out above all else.

For many years I have taught Pattern Drafting in community colleges and in my own school, The Islander School of Fashion Arts. And, always, I have wished for a way to share it with a much wider audience. With the advent of Video the answer was provided. While the subject can certainly be learned from the book, one has to admit it's kind of nice to have a teacher at hand who doesn't object to being wakened in the middle of the night! So, whether with book or video package in hand, let's begin at the beginning.

The subject of this book is, of course, Pant drafting. The most constant lament in sewing is, "I can't get pants to fit!". Small wonder when you glance around at the myriad shapes we human beings come in. It is only necessary to observe 3 people with a hip measurement of 36" to realize how different they can be. The first may be perfectly balanced front to back, the second have a flat hip line and full abdomen, the third a flat abdomen and full hip. Yet, behold how we have attempted to take the same size pattern and "fold, spindle and mutilate" it in an effort to make it fit all three. How much better to create a pattern mirroring the correct proportions. As always, there may be some minor adjustments even when drafting, but they will be minimal in comparison to other methods.

As with any subject you will need to proceed slowly and thoughtfully through your first draft. The method once learned, however, you will find that after doing a few pair you will probably rarely even look at the directions. Accuracy is essential, but the rewards are worth it. I know of no other way to produce as nearly perfect a pant.

We will not be dealing with sewing instructions in this book. It is assumed that most of us who sew have done the construction part before. If not, there are many fine books** available on the market. Our purpose is to produce an accurate pattern.

Enough of the chatter! If you're as excited as I am to get going, grab your tape measure, ruler and pen, don your designer hat and follow me into your "whole new world".

Margaret
Islander

** The publisher recommends Islander Sewing Systems™' book, **"Islander Sewing Systems™ I"** *for Personal and Professional Sewing",* as your main source of basic sewing knowledge. For ordering information see the last page of this publication.

TABLE OF CONTENTS

SUPPLIES

SUPPLIES

1. **Masking Tape**
2. **2 ballpoint pens**, one black, one red (red for corrections)
3. **Reinforced tape measure**
4. **Paper scissors**
5. **1 roll pattern paper.** The very best kind is the examining table paper used in doctors' offices. Be sure to get the glazed type, not the crepe texture, as the crepe textured paper stretches when pressed. Try to get the 21" (53.5 cm) width. Since a wider paper will be needed, you will have to tape two sheets of paper together vertically to get enough width. You can get the paper at a medical supply house or perhaps even from your doctor. Other papers such as newsprint can be used but are not quite as pliable. The recommended kind holds up well over time and is great for tracing commercial multiple size patterns, crafts and all the other things you'll think up! And a roll of it seems to last forever.
6. **1 long ruler**, preferably 45" (115 cm). Steel or aluminum is best.
7. **1 18" (46 cm) C-Thru ruler** with 2" (5 cm) even grid or 1 draftsman's square (again, steel or aluminum is best).
8. **1 hipline curve ruler.** (If this is not available the large plastic curves found in notions departments can be used).
9. **Firmly woven fabric** for the muslin or trial pant. Approx. 2 1/2 yards (2.4 meters) of 45" (115 cm) fabric or 1 1/4 to 1 1/2 yards (1.2 to 1.4 meters) 60" (152.5 cm) fabric.

EQUIPMENT

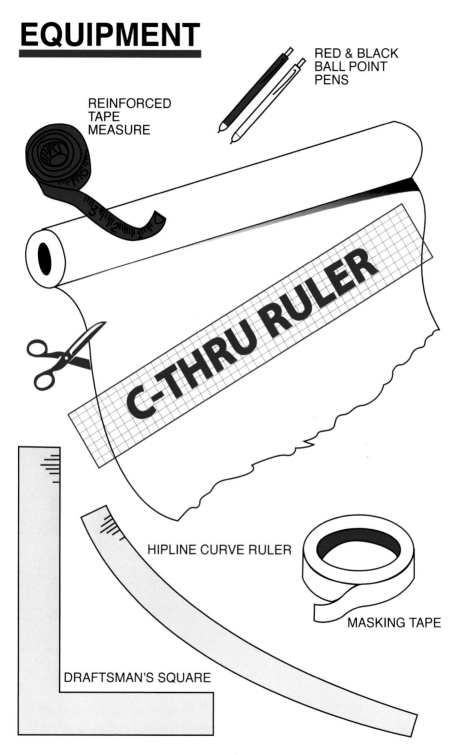

RED & BLACK
BALL POINT
PENS

REINFORCED
TAPE
MEASURE

C-THRU RULER

HIPLINE CURVE RULER

MASKING TAPE

DRAFTSMAN'S SQUARE

HOW TO USE
THE C-THRU RULER

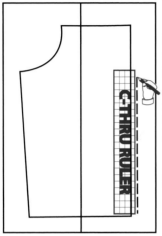

To Add Seam Allowances:
Place ruler lengthwise along edge of pattern extending it from the edge of the pattern the desired amount of seam allowance. Ex: For a 5/8" (1.5 cm) allowance align the edge of the pattern with the lengthwise 5/8" (1.5 cm) line on the ruler, having the 5/8" (1.5 cm) extending out from the pattern. Draw along the edge of the ruler. On curves move the ruler frequently, making small broken lines and blend later.

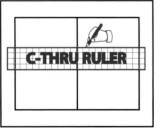

To Square A Line:
Place ruler across the line you are attempting to square, with one of the fine crosswise lines of the ruler resting exactly along the line to be squared. Draw along edge of ruler.*

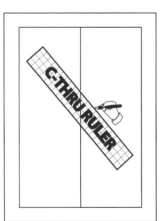

Establishing A Bias Grainline:
Place ruler diagonally across the lengthwise grainline so that the diagonal crosses a 2" section of the ruler. Ex: On one side of the ruler it will rest on 4 and on the other side on 6. Draw along the edge of the ruler to obtain the true bias line. The exact bias measure on a metric ruler may be somewhat different.

As mentioned before, the use of a regular drafting or carpenter's square is perfectly acceptable if you prefer.

MEASURING

NOTES

MEASUREMENT CHART

NOTE: Since we are drafting one half of the pattern, i.e. one leg, most of the horizontal measurements will be divided in half for drafting.

Measurements		Amount	+Ease	Total	1/2
Front waist			1/2"(1.3cm)		
Back waist			1/2"(1.3cm)		
Abdominal Ext.					
Depth at which taken ( )					
Front Hip			1/2"(1.3cm)		
Back Hip			1/2"(1.3cm)		
Depth at which taken ( )					
Crotch depth	(RS)		1/2"(1.3cm)		
	(LS)		to 1"(2.5cm)		
Pant Length	(CF)				
Pant Length	(CB)				
Pant Length	(RS)				
	(LS)				
Knee Length					

In case of very heavy thighs it is advisable to measure the upper leg and record so as to be able to compare with the pant allowance. (There should be 2" (5cm) to 1 1/2" (6.5cm) ease.) The draft normally reflects the correct amount automatically. But, just in case!

On all horizontal measurements above the heavy center line of the chart, the 1/2 measurement will be used throughout the draft. The measurements below the heavy line will be used as recorded.

Abbreviations: CF–Center Front   RS–Right Side
                 CB–Center Back   LS–Left Side

MEASURING

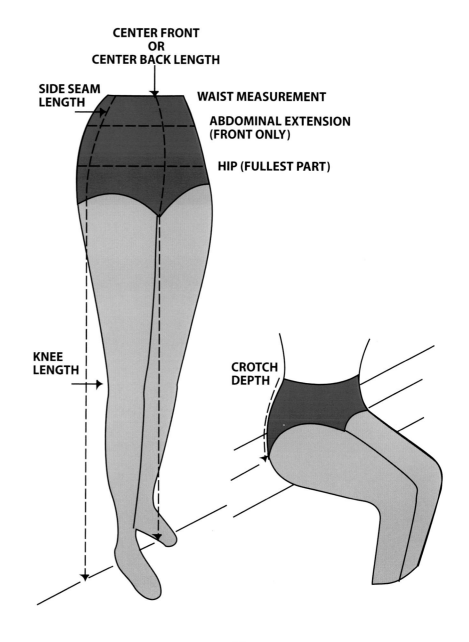

CENTER FRONT OR CENTER BACK LENGTH

SIDE SEAM LENGTH

WAIST MEASUREMENT

ABDOMINAL EXTENSION (FRONT ONLY)

HIP (FULLEST PART)

KNEE LENGTH

CROTCH DEPTH

HOW TO USE
A MEASURING CHART

On the following page open out the extension leaf on which you will find the measuring chart. You will be able to see the chart, diagram and instructions easily while taking your measurements.

Be sure to record your measurements in pencil as you may need to make changes.

As you continue through to completion of your draft leave the chart extended as you turn each page of the directions. In this way you will always have the necessary measurements in full view.

In the probable event you want to draft pants for family, friends, customers, etc. you may want to consider affixing a sheet of tracing paper over the chart in order to have individual charts without damaging the original. For this purpose I find 3M removable magic tape indispensable since it can be peeled off without damaging the surface of the page.

Be sure to label each tracing sheet chart with the name of person and date on which taken and file in a safe place, preferably with the master copy of the completed pant.

CHART

**LEAVE OPEN
WHILE DRAFTING**

TAKING MEASUREMENTS FOR PANTS

CARDINAL RULE FOR MEASURING: Never try to measure yourself. It is practically impossible to do so accurately. Even more importantly, we sometimes get "wishful measurements" when *we* do the job!

For best results, measurements should be taken over garments which will be worn under the finished pant. Accurate results can also be obtained by measuring over a solid leotard. Measuring over street clothes can add too much ease to the finished garment.

Whether measuring is done in bare feet or with shoes is not too important unless one is wearing corrective shoes, in which case measure with shoes on. In the final fitting do wear shoes in order to adjust hemline.

Before starting, use masking tape to mark areas to be measured. A dark line drawn down the center of the tape will make things easier. Place tape or elastic around waist. Place tape down desired side seams and (a small piece of tape) at fullest part of abdomen. With model standing sideways locate the fullest point of hipline and make a crossmark on the sideseam tape. In this same manner mark the length to the knee.

As each measurement is taken, record it in the proper space on your measurement chart, then add to it the amount of ease indicated, if any. (The ease amounts for each area are shown on the measurement chart.) Divide amount in half **if indicated on chart**.

Understandably, some ease is needed for comfortable wearing. This draft calls for an additional 1" (2.5 cm) to be added to the waist and hip measurements. This is adequate in most cases, but if a pant is to be worn over bulky tops, additional ease may be needed. Fitting of the first "muslin" will reveal any necessary adjustments.

WAIST MEASUREMENTS: Wrap tape measure completely around waist, starting precisely at one side seam. Then note which part of the measurement is the front waist. Subtract the front measurement from the total measurement to determine back measurement. Add 1/2" (1.3 cm) ease to each.

ABDOMINAL EXTENSION: Take at the fullest part of the abdomen from side seam to side seam. (Front measurement only!) Usually this is from 3" to 3 ½" (7.5 cm to 9 cm) down from the waist. If very little difference appears between waist and abdomen, use an arbitrary figure of 3" (7.5 cm). Do not pull measuring tape tight, but do not add any additional ease.

HIP MEASUREMENT: Wrap tape measure completely around hip at fullest point, starting precisely at one side seam. Then note which part of the measurement is the front hip. Subtract this amount from the total measurement to determine the back measurement. Add 1/2" (1.3 cm) ease to each. Record depth (down side seam) at which hip measurement was taken.

If front abdominal measurement exceeds hip measurement substitute abdominal measurement for front hip measurement on chart.

PANT LENGTH: Measurement should be taken from the waistline directly to the floor at center front, center back and side seams. Be sure to measure both side seams as there is often a difference. Use the longer measurement for drafting. The difference can be adjusted when sewing.

KNEE LENGTH: Take from the waistline down side seam to the knee.

CROTCH DEPTH: Have person seated on a hard chair or table. Be sure subject is seated comfortably with arms resting naturally at sides. If arms are lifted it lengthens the measurement resulting in too deep a crotchline. Measure from the waistline **over the side seam curve** to the chair. Measure both sides and use the longest measure to draft. To this measurement add 1/2" (1.3 cm) to 1" (2.5 cm) ease depending on the fullness of the hip. The fuller the hip, the more the allowance. I have rarely seen this exceed 3/4" (2 cm), so be conservative on your first draft. 1/2" (1.3 cm) seems average.

NOTE: It is a good idea when you are learning to measure for a draft to take each measurement 3 times. This way you're bound to come up with an average!

NOTES

THE DRAFT

BEFORE YOU START

1. Be sure to work in a well lit area.

2. As with cutting out fabrics, a table which will allow you to stand comfortably upright is a real boon. If your table is not high enough you might consider some large blocks of wood under the legs as a temporary solution. While by no means a necessity, it certainly helps. (Unless you are into self-destruction, the floor is out of the question!)

3. Regarding the drafting paper; many different kinds of paper may be used. You may come up with some originals of your own. However, my favorite is the examination table paper described in the section on SUPPLIES. Since the paper is only 21" (53.5 cm) wide you will need to tape two sheets together lengthwise. Have the paper length about 10" (25.5 cm) to 15" (38 cm) longer than your pant side seam length.

4. You may find it helpful to tape the corners of your paper to the table to prevent slippage.

5. Begin drawing the pattern in the center of the paper.

6. Use a black ballpoint pen with which to draft. This way you have a fine line which is more accurate. Under no circumstances use a felt pen. The thickness of the line itself can add to the size of the garment. The red ballpoint is for correcting any mistakes you make. (For humans only!)

7. Accuracy is the byword in any patternmaking. Not difficult to obtain — just take it slowly the first time and enjoy the new adventure. You'll be surprised at the results.

8. Since it is sometimes difficult to divide a measurement, try using a tried and true shortcut, **"the dressmaker measure"**. Simply cut a narrow strip of paper the length of the line to be divided. If the directions call for dividing the amount in thirds, just fold the strip in thirds and use the resulting amount. If they call for half, fold the strip in half, etc.

9. You will notice as you proceed that the bottom of the pant is always square. Any figure differences will be reflected at the top of the pattern (waistline). Therefore, your pattern will probably appear slightly different at the waistline than the sample and unlike other individual patterns.

IMPORTANT REMINDER

When beginning the draft (page 25) remember that when front waist, back waist, front hip, back hip and abdominal extension measurements are called for they refer to the **1/2** measurements in the right hand column of your measurement chart. (page 15)

STEP ONE

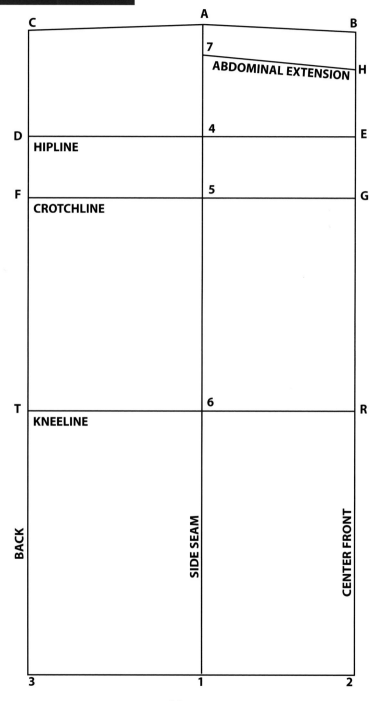

DIRECTIONS

A ➡ 1 = side length

A ➡ 4 = depth at which hip measurement was taken

A ➡ 5 = depth at which crotch measurement was taken

A ➡ 6 = depth at which knee line was measured

Square lines from each of these points. At this point you need only square a short distance each side of the side seam line. The following steps will complete the exact distance of these crosslines.

4 ➡ E = front hip measurement

4 ➡ D = back hip measurement

(3 ➡ 1 ➡ 2) = (D ➡ 4 ➡ E)

3 ➡ C = back length squared from 3 (Simply place a ruler from 3 through D to square)

2 ➡ B = front length squared from 2

Top of pant will usually be uneven, reflecting sway back, high hip, etc.

Connect C ➡ A ➡ B

A ➡ 7 = depth at which abdominal extension was measured

B ➡ H = A ➡ 7   Connect H ➡ 7

Label all points as shown on diagram.

STEP TWO

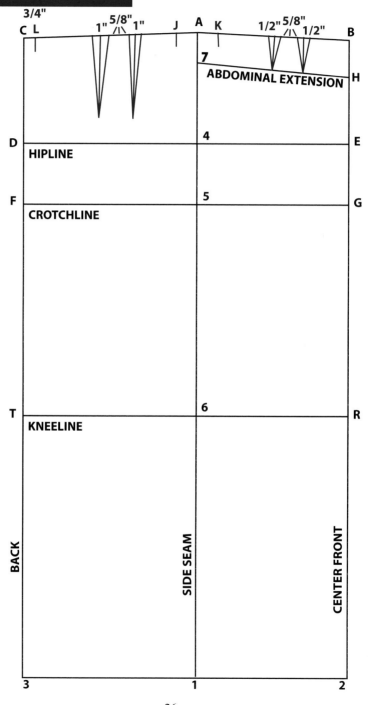

3/4"

C L · · · 1" 5/8" 1" · J · A · K · 1/2" 5/8" 1/2" · B

7

ABDOMINAL EXTENSION · H

D · 4 · E

HIPLINE

F · 5 · G

CROTCHLINE

T · 6 · R

KNEELINE

BACK

SIDE SEAM

CENTER FRONT

3 · 1 · 2

DIRECTIONS

C ➡ L = 3/4" (2 cm)

DARTS:

L ➡ J = back waist measurement + 2" (5 cm)

B ➡ K= front waist measurement + 1" (2.5 cm)

** Don't panic if there is not a surplus of 2"(5 cm) in back or 1" (2.5 cm) in front left over. See note ** on next page.

Locate and mark center of L ➡ J and B ➡ K

Mark 5/8" (1.5 cm) each side of center mark to begin darts.

(Dart position may be changed later to suit individual tastes.)

Back darts: Mark off 1" (2.5 cm) away from each 5/8" (1.5 cm) mark.

Front darts: Mark off 1/2" (1.3 cm) away from each 5/8" (1.5 cm) mark.

Square a line through center of each dart, parallel to Center Front and Center Back, 5 to 6 inches long (12.5 to 15 cm) for back darts. Ex: If back hip depth measure is 8" (20 cm) make the dart length 6" (15 cm). Extend front darts to abdominal extension line. (Usually 3" (7.5 cm))

Connect legs of darts to center line.

**

NOTE: If waist and hip measurement are nearly the same you may not have excess to form the darts. Of the amount that does remain use a small portion of the excess from **A ➜ J** (or **A ➜ K**). Use the remaining amount for darts.

Ex: If 1¼" (3.2 cm) remains in back, use 1/4" (6mm) from **A ➜ J** and remainder to form two 1/2" (1.3 cm) darts.

If 3/4" (2 cm) remains in back, use 1/4" (6mm) from **A ➜ K** and remainder to form two 1/4" (6mm) darts.

If amount remaining is too small for 2 darts, make a single dart in the center of the piece.

Some pant patterns need no darts other than for esthetic reasons.

If no excess remains for front darts, yet they are needed for styling purposes, see **Additional Notes** (page 47).

NOTES

STEP THREE

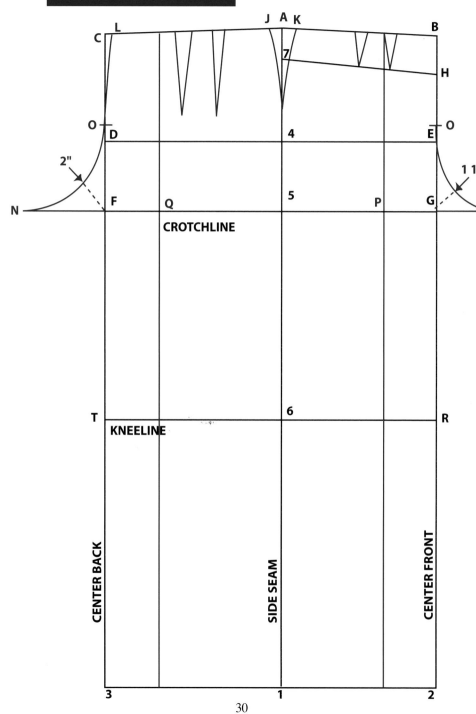

DIRECTIONS

Using a hipline curve ruler, draw a curved line from each of points **J** and **K** to blend in just below abdominal extension line. After drawing hip curves remeasure abdominal extension line to make sure it remains adequate. If **J** ➡ **7** and **K** ➡ **7** are dissimilar curves they may be corrected.
See **Additional Notes**.

Mark Points **O** approx. 1 ½" (3.8 cm) above **D** and **E**.

Connect **L** to **O**.

CROTCH:

> (The "dressmaker measure" on page 23 will be helpful in this section.)
>
> **G** ➡ **M** = 1/3 of **5** ➡ **G** extended out
>
> **F** ➡ **N** = 1/2 of **5** ➡ **F** extended out
>
> **G** ➡ **P** = **G** ➡ **M**
>
> **F** ➡ **Q** = **G** ➡ **P**
>
> NOTE: The only time the 1/2 measure is used is for the back crotch extension.
>
> Square vertical lines from **P** and **Q** for crease lines.

FRONT CROTCH CURVE:

> Draw a diagonal line approx. 1½" (3.8 cm) long from **G** as a guideline for crotch curve. Draw in curve from **O** to **M**.

BACK CROTCH CURVE:

Draw a diagonal line approx. 2" (5 cm) long from **F** as a guideline for crotch curve. Draw in curve from **O** to **N**.

TO DRAW CURVES:

If you are artistic, wing it! If not, use a french curve or trace the crotch curve of a similar size commerical pattern for a template.

NOTES

STEP FOUR
TO COMPLETE PANT

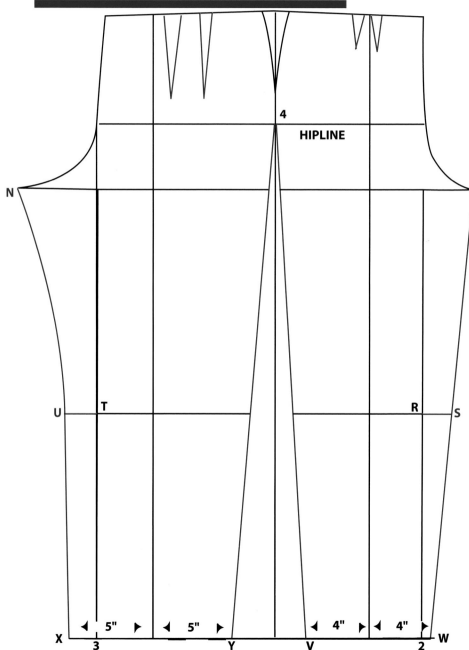

DIRECTIONS

Mark off 1/2 of desired bottom width of front on either side of front grainline. Mark **V** and **W**.

Mark off 1/2 of desired bottom width of back on either side of crease line. (Back is usually 1" (2.5 cm) more each side of crease line than front.) Mark **X** and **Y**.

FRONT: Connect **M ➡ W**
Connect **V ➡ 4** (hipline)
Connect **Y ➡ 4** (hipline)
Measure **R ➡ S**

BACK: **T ➡ U = R ➡ S**
Connect **N ➡ U** with a slight curve
Connect **U ➡ X**

If indentation at **U** is too sharp straighten the curve slightly.

Compare measurement of **M ➡ W** and **N ➡ X**. Correct any discrepancy by lowering crotch line at point **N**.

Trace finished patterns onto a fresh sheet of paper and add seam allowances. See **Additional Notes** (page 47).

Be sure to trace grainline (creaseline), darts and kneeline.

If unsure of your bottom pant width, try the measurements shown on our sample draft for your first pattern.

Once again, your draft may look slightly different than the sample.

Be sure, after tracing the pattern, that you preserve your original draft. This way if the tracing is lost or damaged, you can retrace.

TRACING FINISHED PATTERN AND ADDING SEAM ALLOWANCES

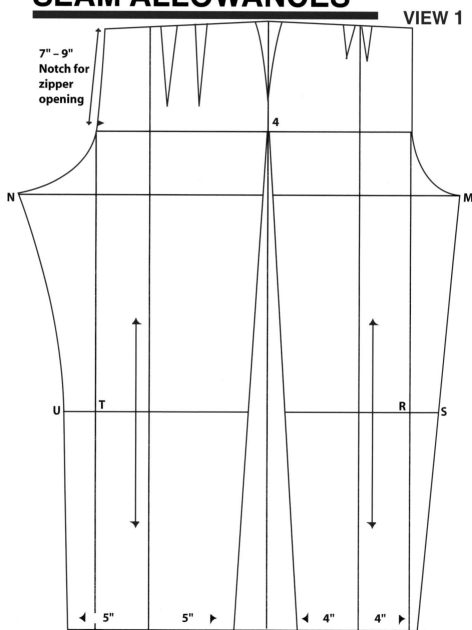

7" – 9"
Notch for
zipper
opening

4

N

M

U T

R S

5"

5"

4"

4"

DIRECTIONS

Trace back and front patterns, separately, from the original draft. See highlighted draft illustration. **(View 1)**

Be sure to mark in darts, grainline (creaseline) and kneeline. You may wish to mark in crotchline and hipline if needed for other styles.

Add desired seam allowances. (See pg. 10 on using the C-Thru ruler to do this.) Notch for zipper 7" – 9" down.

No extra allowance for a hem is necessary on the trial pant since the measurements were taken to the floor. This will leave some extra allowance at the hemline.

Before cutting out side seams of finished pattern, fold up hem allowance. Since the pant usually is tapered, this will allow the hem to fit to the pant when folded up. See illustration. **(View 2)**

Before cutting pattern at waistline seam, fold out darts in the direction they will be pressed when sewing. This results in the shaping you usually see on dart patterns which allows the dart to fit the curve of the waistline when sewn. See illustration. **(View 3)**

VIEW 2   **VIEW 3**

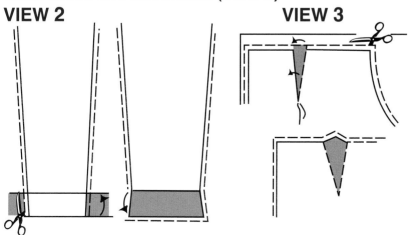

FOR A MORE
FITTED PANT

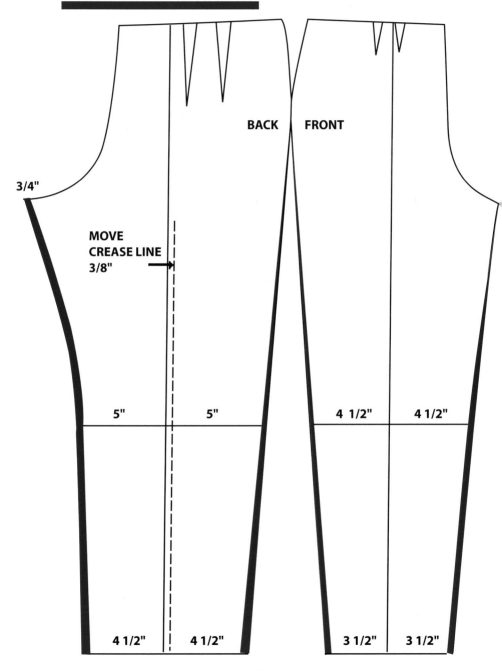

BACK   FRONT

3/4"

MOVE
CREASE LINE
3/8"

5"   5"   4 1/2"   4 1/2"

4 1/2"   4 1/2"   3 1/2"   3 1/2"

DIRECTIONS

The original draft produces a trouser like pant. "Kathryn Hepburn" look! To achieve a more fitted pant which cups under the back hipline, make the following adjustments to the pattern.

Move the creaseline of back 3/8" (1 cm) toward the side seam.

Shorten back crotch by 3/4" (2 cm).

Adjust width of leg at knee and hem as shown, blending to crotchline and hipline. Amounts used here are suggested amounts only. However, in most cases, be sure front and back measurements are kept in the same balance.

If you are trying for a very narrow ankle when experimenting with new designs, be sure that you are still able to get your foot through the opening! I once designed the slimmest, best looking pant line. However, when graded down to a size 8 no one could get the pant on. A size 8 can, of course, have a size 10 foot!

After shortening back crotch, if crotch seems to pull, add the 3/4" back in at the crotch and taper to new style line a few inches down.

WAISTBANDS

When total waist, front waist or back waist measurements are used be sure to use the measurements given on your chart **without** added ease.

NOTE: If you have compensated at the side seams to even up the curves, you will need to adjust the front and back waist measurements accordingly. (A very minor amount). See **Additional Notes** chapter (page 47).

WAISTBAND: CENTER BACK OPENING

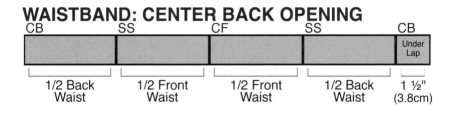

CB	SS	CF	SS	CB
1/2 Back Waist	1/2 Front Waist	1/2 Front Waist	1/2 Back Waist	1 ½" (3.8cm)

Draw a rectangle the total measurement of the waistline and two times the desired finished width. (I like most waistbands to finish off at 1 ¼" (3.2 cm) so I draw a 2 ½" (6.5 cm) rectangle.) Find the exact center of the rectangle and mark this **CF** (center front). On each side of this point mark off 1/2 the front waist measurement. Mark these points **SS** (side seam). The amounts remaining between the **SS** and ends of the rectangle on each side should be 1/2 the back waist measurement. Mark ends of rectangle **CB** (center back). At one end of the band (whichever is the intended underlap) add 1 ½" (3.8 cm) for the underlap. Complete by adding seam allowances all around.

WAISTBAND: SIDE SEAM OPENING

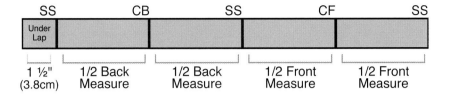

SS	CB	SS	CF	SS
1 ½" (3.8cm)	1/2 Back Measure	1/2 Back Measure	1/2 Front Measure	1/2 Front Measure

Draw rectangle as above, then place markings as
follows: Mark the right-hand edge of the rectangle
SS. To the left of this point mark off 1/2 the front waist
measurement (from chart). Mark this point **CF**. From
CF left mark off 1/2 the front waist measurement again.
Mark this point **SS**. From this point left, mark off 1/2 the
back waist measurement. Mark this point **CB**. From
this point left, mark off 1/2 the back waist measurement
again. Mark this point **SS**. From this point left, add 1 ½"
(3.8 cm) for an underlap. Add seam allowances.

WAISTBAND: CENTER FRONT OPENING

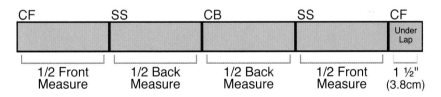

CF	SS	CB	SS	CF
1/2 Front Measure	1/2 Back Measure	1/2 Back Measure	1/2 Front Measure	1 ½" (3.8cm)

Draw rectangle as above, then place markings as
follows: Mark each end of rectangle **CF**. Starting at
right side of rectangle mark off (to the left) 1/2 the front
waist measurement. Mark this point **SS**. From this point
left, mark off 1/2 the back waist measurement. Mark
this point **CB**. From **CB** left, mark off 1/2 back waist

measurement again. Mark this point **SS**. From this point left, mark off 1/2 front waist measurement. Mark this point **CF**. On right hand side of band add 1 ½" (3.8 cm) for an underlap. Add seam allowances.

ELASTIC WAIST

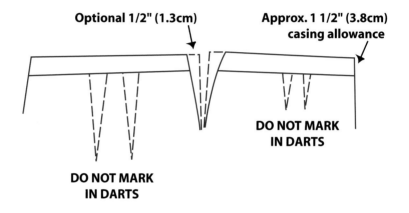

Optional 1/2" (1.3cm)

Approx. 1 1/2" (3.8cm) casing allowance

DO NOT MARK IN DARTS

DO NOT MARK IN DARTS

While you should not use an elastic waistband for your first fitting pair of pants, you may later wish to use one. The method is really quite simple. In most cases, just do not mark in darts when tracing pattern. Then add the amount needed above the waistline for a casing. (Usually 1 ½" (3.8 cm)) In rare cases you may want to add approximately 1/2 " (1.3 cm) at the side seams and taper into the abdominal extension point.

THE MUSLIN
or
TRIAL PANT

SUGGESTIONS FOR MAKING THE MUSLIN OR TRIAL PANT

Remember that this first muslin is a straight legged pant which you may like or may later wish to narrow. Our object in this muslin is to make sure we have a great fit in the trunk of the pant. The legs are styled later *if* you choose.

Always make the trial pant up in a firm muslin or similar fabric to test the pattern. If you purchase some "bargain table" brushed denim, chino, etc, you will probably be able to wear the finished trial pant. But, just in case you're human, don't buy silk or linen for the first try! Do not use double knit for your trial pant. After perfecting your firmly woven muslin you can usually use the pattern equally well for a firm double knit, but the reverse is not true.

In constructing the muslin, join the side seams, then the inseams. Place one leg inside the other and join the crotch seam. Trim the crotch seam down to 1/4" (6 mm) in the curved area before trying on. I often hear, "I don't want to trim it until I see if it's going to fit". Do not attach waistband until after the trial fitting.

In constructing the pant make sure your seam allowances are sewn accurately. Use tracing paper to mark them if necessary. Accuracy is imperative!

Before trying on the finished muslin carefully press open

all seams excepting the crotch curve.

Be sure to try the muslin on right side out. Most people have slight variations from one side to the other. This way you will see the pant as it will be worn.

The lower edge of the pant should be folded up for the try-on in order to allow the pant to hang straight down.

When trying on the muslin, tie a piece of 1/4" (6 mm) elastic firmly around waistline and adjust pant to body. Make sure side seams are hanging straight (plumb) to the floor. In the event your two side seam measurements differed, you will undoubtedly have an excess above the elastic on one side. Trim the excess off the muslin and record its measurement for future use along with a notation of which side it was trimmed from. **(Since this is only a one side adjustment, do not take the amount off the pant pattern.)** In this manner you will know by your notes when making future pants, that you remove the recorded amount from that side during the sewing process.

OTHER ADJUSTMENTS: In the first try-on you may notice the need for minor adjustments. (Remember, the pattern exactly reflects the accuracy of the measurements taken!) If you note that the hipline is a little full or the waistline a little high at the side seams, for example, you can usually correct it on the pattern itself by trimming it a little, etc. However, when you make the correction, immediately remeasure the body in that area and record the correct amount on your measurement chart. This way if you decide to redraft, you do so with correct figures.

(Once again a reminder. When an adjustment is made to only one side of the pant, it is corrected in sewing the garment, not on the pattern.)

If your first pattern appears to need a great deal of adjustment, it is really easier to take the measurements over again and do another draft. *And,* the second time, it's more familiar and really fun to do. Try to ascertain from the incorrect muslin which areas need correction before remeasuring. (i.e. Was the center front too short, side seam too long, etc?)

Be sure to leave an opening in back or front to try on. Don't laugh – everyone does it once.

ADDITIONAL NOTES

NOTES

TO COMPENSATE HIPLINE CURVES

If hipline curves **J** ➡ **7** and **K** ➡ **7** appear too dissimilar they can easily be corrected. Simply measure the distance from **J** to **K**. Then divide this amount in half and mark off 1/2 each side of line **A** and redraw curves to point **7**.

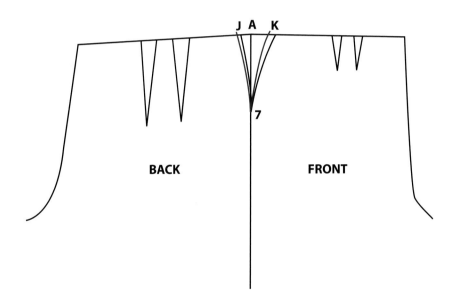

FRONT DART CHANGES

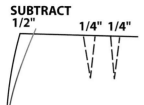

SUBTRACT
1/2"

1/4" 1/4"

VIEW 1
TO REMOVE FRONT DARTS

With very few exceptions the darts are only removed in the front of the pant. The back darts are essential to correctly fit the greater back difference between waist and hip. There are various reasons for wanting to remove front darts such as wanting a smoother front look. Also it is sometimes convenient when changing a style-line, as in adding pleats, not to have to work around the darts. If the darts are not more than 1/4" deep (6 mm) use the following method. If the darts are, for example, 1/2" deep (1.3 cm) the most desirable fit will be obtained by leaving one dart in the pant and removing the other by the following method.

First make a tracing of the original draft so as to preserve the original pattern. Do not add seam allowance to tracing until pattern is completed.

Take off 1/2" (1.3 cm) on the sideseam at the waistline and taper to nothing at abdominal extension. After removing the excess, simply eliminate the original darts, or one of the two if they are 1/2" (1.3 cm) from the finished pattern.

ADD
1/2:   1/4" 1/4"

VIEW 2
TO ADD FRONT DARTS

If your pattern does not have front darts, due to a minimal difference between waist and abdomen, you can still achieve the look of front darts with very little effort. Simply add 1/2" (1.3 cm) to the sideseam at the waistline and taper to nothing at the abdominal extension. Then draw in two 1/4" (6 mm) darts, centering them on the pant pattern and making them about 3" (7.5 cm) long. Be sure to fold out the darts before cutting the waistline of the pattern.

VIEW 3
TO MINIMIZE ABDOMEN

Optical illusion plays a great part in designing clothing. Here is one illusion we have found really works in disguising a full abdomen. Since front darts can be moved about with considerable freedom, just draw in 2 new darts on your tracing at angles similar to those shown. Measure the total width of the two original darts and divide this amount so as to create a longer and wider dart nearest center front and a shorter, narrower dart toward the side seam. Be sure to fold out the darts before cutting the waistline of pattern.

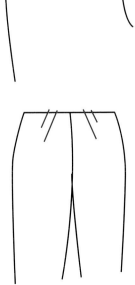

DRAFTING FOR THE ASYMMETRICAL FIGURE

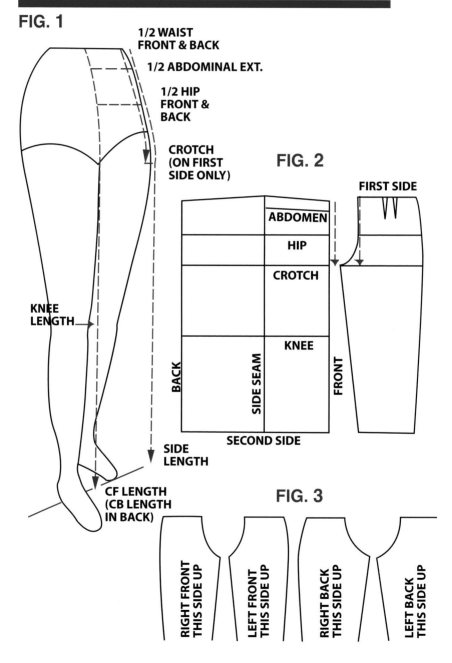

FIG. 1

1/2 WAIST FRONT & BACK

1/2 ABDOMINAL EXT.

1/2 HIP FRONT & BACK

CROTCH (ON FIRST SIDE ONLY)

KNEE LENGTH

SIDE LENGTH

CF LENGTH (CB LENGTH IN BACK)

FIG. 2

FIRST SIDE

ABDOMEN

HIP

CROTCH

KNEE

BACK

SIDE SEAM

FRONT

SECOND SIDE

FIG. 3

RIGHT FRONT THIS SIDE UP

LEFT FRONT THIS SIDE UP

RIGHT BACK THIS SIDE UP

LEFT BACK THIS SIDE UP

DIRECTIONS

Occasionally we find, due to an accident, etc., a figure is markedly different on one side from the other. While most normal figure discrepancies can be handled in the regular draft with minor correction in the sewing process, this problem is best resolved by doing a separate draft for each side of the body. For the person with this problem who has never been able to buy or wear pants this method is an absolute gem!

The concept is really simple. Just do the draft as you did for the original except that you measure each side as though it were two people and do a separate draft for each side. (Remember, we were doing a half draft, anyway.) Following are the directions:

When taping, clearly mark the center front and center back seams to be sure the figure is divided in half. Do remainder of taping as for the original draft.

THE FOLLOWING MEASUREMENTS ARE TAKEN FOR EACH SIDE SEPARATELY:

Measure 1/2 the front waist and 1/2 the back waist.

Measure 1/2 the front abdominal measurement and depth.

Measure 1/2 the front hip and 1/2 the back hip and depth.

Measure side seam to floor on the same side.

Measure crotch depth only on side being drafted first (note following).

THE MEASUREMENTS BELOW ARE COMMON TO BOTH SIDES:

Measure center front to floor.
Measure center back to floor.
Locate depth of knee on center front line (**instead of on side seam**).

DRAFTING FIRST HALF

Use measurements from only one side.

Proceed with draft as per original drafting instructions, including crotch depth, with the following exceptions. Mark in knee line **after** drawing in center front line. (The knees have to be across from each other!) Complete draft.

DRAFTING SECOND HALF

Use second set of measurements.

Do not mark in crotch depth line on the draft for this side until center front line is drawn in. **NOTE: On the already completed half pattern,** measure down the **center front** line to the crotchline (Fig. 1) and use that figure to locate the crotch depth on the **CENTER FRONT** line of the half you are now doing. (Fig. 2)

Complete patterns, being sure to copy all markings when tracing.

IMPORTANT

Mark each half pattern as follows:

**Right Front – This Side Up Left Front – This Side Up
Right Back – This Side Up Left Back – This Side Up**

This way when you lay the pattern out you will be sure to have it right side up on the fabric. (Fig 3)

A SUGGESTED ADJUSTMENT FOR A VERY HEAVY HIPLINE

I have sometimes found this a helpful pattern adjustment where the back hip width was so extreme as to cause the back pant leg to appear too wide.

After completing regular pant pattern, narrow each side of back leg an additional 1/2" (1.3 cm) on each side at bottom. Continue taking off the same amount until about 2" (5 cm) to 3" (7.5 cm) above the knee. Then taper to nothing at the crotchline on the inseam and to the hipline on the outseam.

If possible try this one in a muslin first to determine the individual fit.

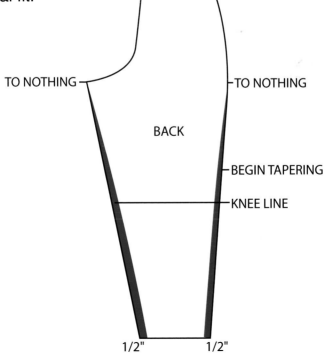

NOTES

Variations

FLY FRONT PLACKET

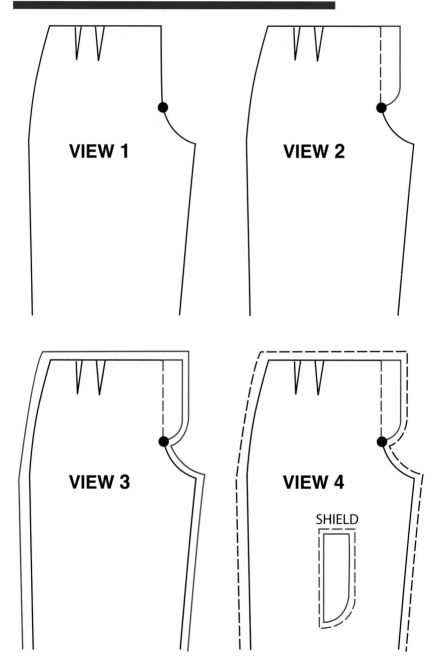

VIEW 1

VIEW 2

VIEW 3

VIEW 4

SHIELD

DIRECTIONS

Draw fly front variation before adding seam allowances to pattern.

Establish length desired for opening. Do not allow placket to extend into the curved area of the crotch. Place a dot on Center Front at lower end of placket. **(VIEW 1)**

Draw a 1 ¼" (3.2 cm) line parallel to Center Front curving in at lower edge to connect with the dot. **(VIEW 2)**

Add seam allowances to the pattern.

Draw a broken line from the dot to the top of the pant on the stitching line. (Center Front). This will indicate the basting line when constructing the pant. **(VIEW 3)**

The 1 ¼" (3.2 cm) width for the fly facing is a suggestion. It may be widened slightly for design purposes if desired.

If a shield is desired a pattern can be made by tracing the front fly extension from the center front line to the edge as illustrated. When cutting out garment, cut 2 shield pieces. **(VIEW 4)**

TO ADD A SINGLE FRONT PLEAT

VIEW 1
IF YOU HAVE NO FRONT DARTS
(Or have removed two 1/4" (6 mm) darts.)

Trace the front leg of the pant. Do not add seam allowances.

Draw a line from desired placement for a pleat at the waistline to the center of the leg at the lower edge.

Slash this line from the waistline to within 1/8" (3 mm) of the lower edge. Spread the opening at the top the amount desired for the pleat. (2" (5 cm) would be a good trial amount.) Trace down each edge of slash opening for approximately 3" (7.5 cm). Trace around remainder of pant. Remove "working sloper" (the one that was slashed). Add seam allowances to the pattern. Square a new grainline from bottom of pant. The space between the 3" (7.5 cm) lines is your pleat. Be sure to fold out pleat, bringing 3" (7.5 cm) guidelines together before cutting waistline edge of the pattern. Fold pleat in the direction it will later be pressed.

Note: If you have one remaining 1/2" (1.3 cm) dart, follow the above directions. You will have a pleat with a dart to the side.

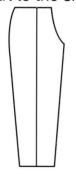
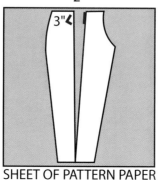
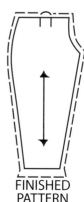

2"

3"

SHEET OF PATTERN PAPER

FINISHED PATTERN

VIEW 2
TO ADD TWO PLEATS

If you have no darts or have removed them both, locate desired placement for the pleats. From these two points draw straight lines to the center of the lower edge of the pant. Slash both lines and spread each slash the amount desired for the pleat. Mark down each edge of each slash approximately 3" (7.5 cm). Trace around entire pant. Square a new grainline from bottom of pant. Add seam allowances and complete as in previous pattern.

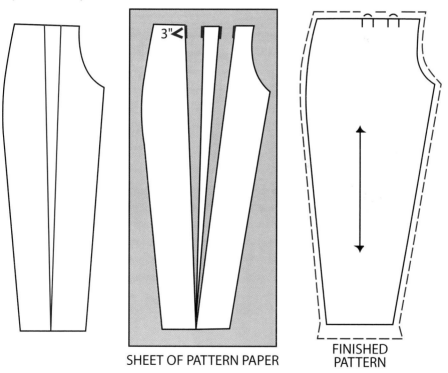

SHEET OF PATTERN PAPER

FINISHED PATTERN

VIEW 3
TO ADD PLEATS WITHOUT
REMOVING DARTS

When drawing slash lines as in previous examples draw lines through center of one or both darts depending on desired number of pleats. Draw slash lines from center of darts at waistline straight through tip of darts to center of lower edge of pant. Slash lines and mark down 3" (7.5 cm) each side of slash as before. Trace pattern and add seam allowances. Square a new grainline from bottom of pant. Before folding out pleats widen each side of each pleat by 1/2 the width of the dart it replaced. Ex: If the original dart was 1/2" (1.3 cm), widen the pleat by 1/4" (6 mm) each side of the pleat. In this way the waistline will be returned to its original size.

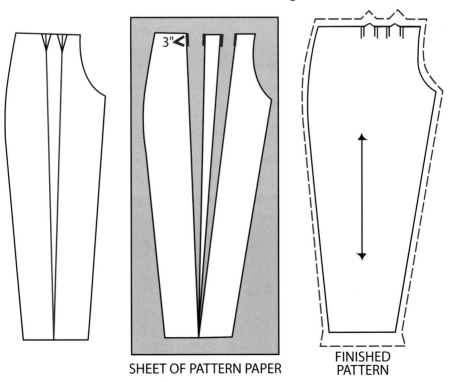

SHEET OF PATTERN PAPER

FINISHED
PATTERN

POCKETS

Here are two of the most commonly used pant pockets. They will get you started. However, if you have commercial patterns with pockets you would like to use, you can usually just overlay them on your pattern and trace them off, adjusting them to your pattern where necessary.

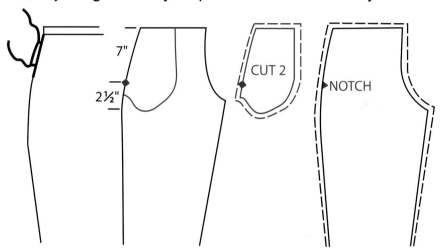

VIEW 1
SIDE OPENING POCKET

Make pocket pattern before adding seam allowances.

Draw in pocket on pant pattern as shown.

Place notch at end of pocket opening.

Trace off outline of pocket piece to form pocket pattern, being sure to mark in notch on both pocket and pant.

Add seam allowances to all pieces.

When cutting out pant in fabric, cut 2 pocket pieces for each pocket.

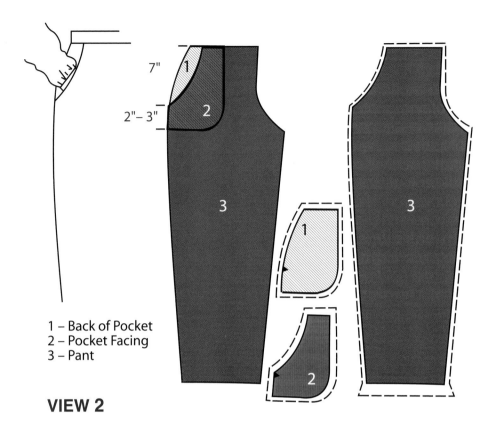

7"

2"– 3"

1 – Back of Pocket
2 – Pocket Facing
3 – Pant

VIEW 2

Make pocket pattern before adding seam allowances.

Draw in pocket on pant pattern as shown.

Trace off individual pocket and pant sections as pictured, being sure to notch pocket back as well as pant.

Add seam allowances to all pieces.

When cutting pant out of fabric, cut 1 of each pocket piece for each pocket.

SOME APPROXIMATE
PANT LENGTHS

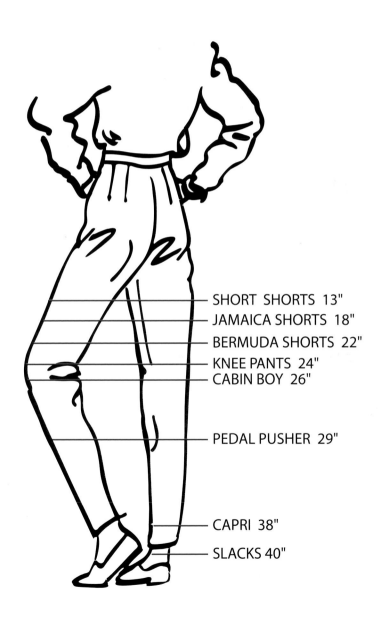

SHORT SHORTS 13"
JAMAICA SHORTS 18"
BERMUDA SHORTS 22"
KNEE PANTS 24"
CABIN BOY 26"

PEDAL PUSHER 29"

CAPRI 38"

SLACKS 40"